I0626894

My Little Greek Book *of Food*

Φαγητά

(fa-gee-TÁ)

ISBN: 979-8-9994762-0-3

Written & Illustrated by: Cali Stefanos

mylittlegreekbook.com

Μήλο

(MEE-lo) • Apple

Μπανάνα

(ba-NÁ-na) • Banana

Αχλάδι

(ah-HLÁ-thee) • Pear

Φράουλα

(FRÁ-ou-la) • Strawberry

Ροδάκινο

(ro-DÁ-kee-no) • Peach

Κεράσια

(ke-RÁ-sia) • Cherries

Καρπούζι

(kar-POU-zee) • Watermelon

Σταφύλια

(sta-FEE-lya) • Grapes

Πορτοκάλι

(por-to-KÁ-lee) • Orange

Ανανάς

(ah-na-NÁS) • Pineapple

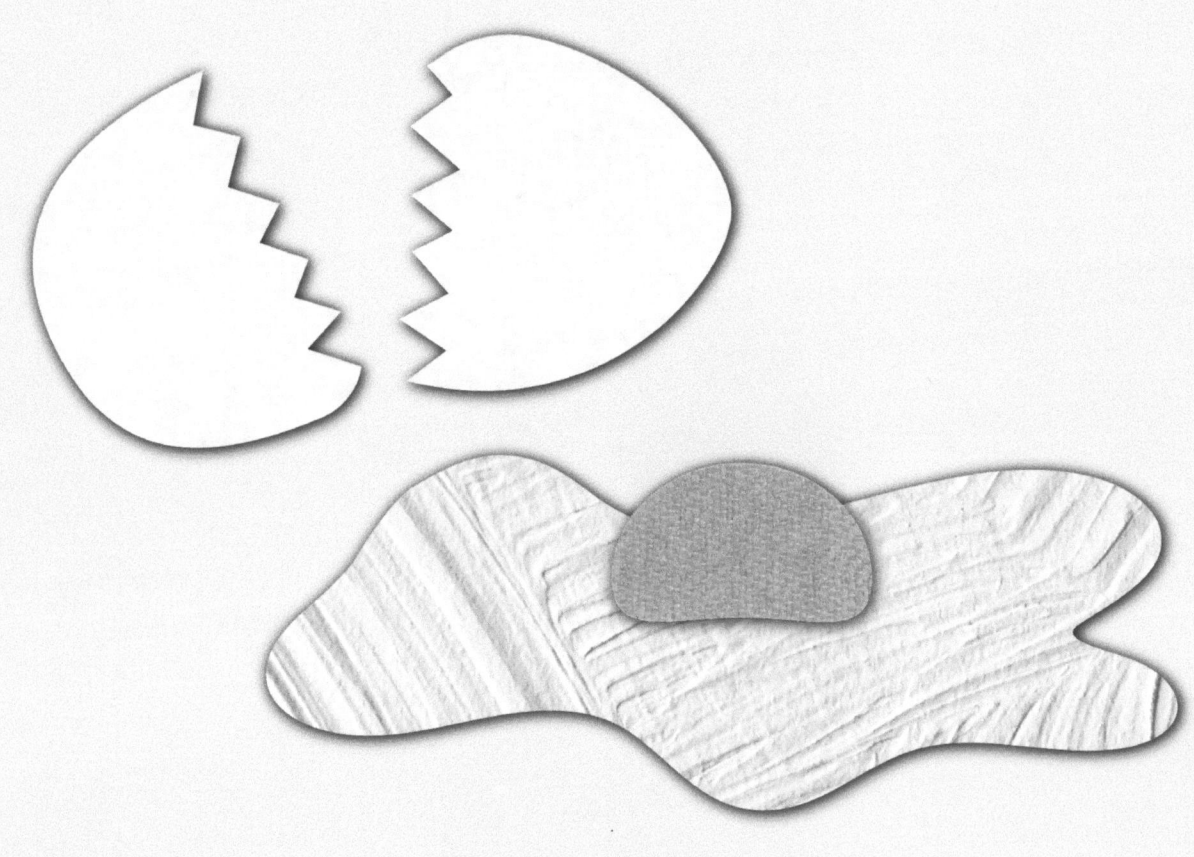

Αυγó

(av-GÓ) • Egg

Ψωμί

(pso-MEE) • Bread

Ρύζι

(REE-zee) • Rice

Tupí

(tee-REE) • Cheese

Μέλι

(MEH-lee) • Honey

Γιαούρτι

(yah-OOR-tee) • Yogurt

Μπρόκολο

(BRO-ko-lo) • Broccoli

Ελιές

(e-lyEs) • Olives

Καρότο

(ka-RO-to) • Carrot

Ντομάτα

(do-MÁ-ta) • Tomato

Πιπεριά

(pee-per-YÁ) • Bell Pepper

Αγγούρι

(ah-GOO-ree) • Cucumber